Winter Blossoms

Winter Blossoms

✦

and other poems

Mamata Misra

Illustrated by Indira Chakravorty

iUniverse, Inc.
New York Lincoln Shanghai

Winter Blossoms
and other poems

Copyright © 2007 by Mamata Misra

iUniverse books may be ordered through booksellers or by contacting:

iUniverse
2021 Pine Lake Road, Suite 100
Lincoln, NE 68512
www.iuniverse.com
1-800-Authors (1-800-288-4677)

ISBN: 978-0-595-44372-7 (pbk)
ISBN: 978-0-595-88701-9 (ebk)

Printed in the United States of America

To my family:

Jayadev
Amitav
Anuj
April

Contents

Foreword

Mamata Misra's *Winter Blossoms* represents a cross cultural journey that not only explores the experiences of South Asian women, but also reflects all women's connection with everything and everyone around them. From arranged marriages to a mother's delight for her unborn children, Mamata's clear, compassionate voice echoes the bittersweet quality of women's lives. Like her poem "Rollercoaster," she takes us on an adventure filled with the complexities of living and dying. I recommend that readers fasten their seat belts. You're in for one amazing ride.

K.J. Wilson, Ed.D.
10/29/06

Dr. Wilson, an accomplished speaker and trainer, is the author of *When Violence Begins At Home: A Comprehensive Guide to Understanding and Ending Domestic Abuse* (2005 & 1997) and a contributing author in *Family Violence: Current Controversies* (2001).

Preface

In *Winter Blossoms*, Mamata Misra gifts us, readers, with a bouquet of poems that would touch every soul. It is a collection that has emerged out of the poet's life experiences—migration to a distant land, motherhood without tradition, anti-domestic violence activism, and above all, being a woman in a world where female ethos carry little value. The poems chart Mamata's growth, her development into a maturity that has overcome everyday barriers and boundaries of conventional restrictions. Mamata's poet eyes see misunderstanding and anguish, injustice and abuse, and her spirited mind questions their inevitability. Mamata is indignant at the cruelties of life; yet, she writes with a heart filled with compassion. At times she is wistful and nostalgic, and at others, righteous and challenging; but at all times Mamata is caring and forgiving. The voice that materializes in *Winter Blossoms* is not shrill, nor diffident and retiring—it is a tender and assertive voice that is clear as a bell.

In *Winter Blossoms*, Mamata states, asks, and seeks. Faces of battered women, abandoned wives, bewildered daughters, and defeated mothers peep out of the lines of her poems. We see them, their conditions, and Mamata Misra compels us to question, "why?" Nevertheless, *Winter Blossoms* is not just about dishonor, loss, and grief. Ultimately, Mamata's words call us to interrogate human indignity, hostility, and domination and then she whispers in our ear: "change, change, change." She takes us gently by the hand and leads us to hope.

Winter Blossoms is courageous and bold, like the buds that dare to bloom in the dead of a freezing season. The truths in *Winter Blossoms* go beyond the limitations of a particular community and reach the universal.

Shamita Das Dasgupta
12/6/06

Shamita Das Dasgupta, an activist and writer, is the cofounder of Manavi, Inc. She is a coauthor of *The Demon Slayer and Other Stories: Bengali Folktales* (1995) and the editor of *A Patchwork Shawl: Chronicles of South Asian Women in America* (1998) and *Body evidence: Intimate violence against South Asian women in America* (2007).

Introduction

I was born and raised in India. I migrated to the US in 1973 to join my husband. The geographical separation from my family and culture was a new experience. Writing became a necessity for me to stay in touch with my folks and to get to know my new family acquired through marriage. As I grew and gathered new experiences, writing remained with me as a trusted companion to provide relief when the heart seemed too full or the stomach churned. I can't deny writing from the head, but I have been more pleased with the pieces that came out of my heart, when the writing was in charge of me rather than I being in charge of the writing.

The poems in this book were written during the period 1993-2006, when I raised my children, took care of ill extended family members, volunteered as an advocate for battered women and their children through an organization called SAHELI in Austin, Texas and discovered and admired wisdom in Vedantic scriptures from ancient India. Naturally, the poems were inspired by the abundance of feelings and thoughts that rose out of the situations and experiences of people around me. Some of the poems made their way into various magazines, journals, poetry reading events, and non-profit newsletters and found appreciative readers, who encouraged me to publish a book. When I decided to publish a book and looked at the poems I had written, five themes emerged.

The first of these themes is **Mother and Child**. Raising our children in a culture foreign to us and not having our parents around to understand, guide, and help was a learning experience with its challenges for South Asians of my generation in the US. My interactions with battered women with children made me aware of the additional problems they faced in raising their children as single mothers. Poems in the first group express some of these thoughts.

The second theme is **War and Peace.** Anti-violence advocates saw war and sought peace not just in the conventional way but at various levels: there was interpersonal violence, racial or communal violence, terrorism, and war against terror, each affecting people around us.

Often questions arose for which there weren't apparent answers. But it seemed important to raise the questions anyway, at least in poetry, leading to the theme **Questions not Answers.**

While working with victims and survivors of domestic violence I saw hope and despair playing hide and seek in their minds, as they walked the maze of life going forward and backward again and again. Poems that were born out of the associated tossing and turning are grouped under the theme **Hope and Despair.**

I had, by this period, crossed the first half of my life. Members of my extended family were growing old and dying. Life's excitements were producing sounds of all sorts and death or trauma's humbling silence was neutralizing them. Vedantic studies were offering new ways to look at life and death in their own merit, without embellishments. I grouped the poems about different aspects of living and dying into the theme **Sound and Silence.**

I have included the time of composition, acknowledgment of previous publication, explanation of non-English words, mythological names used, and other anecdotal information about each poem in the section "Poems" at the end of this book. For previously published poems mentioned, I would like to acknowledge the editors of the *SAHELI Newletter*, *South Asian Women's Forum* (www.sawf.org) webzine, *Asian American Quarterly*, *Scribe* of the Austin Writer's League, Journal of the Orissa Society of the Americas, Journal and Newsletter of the Austin Chinmaya Mission, *Volunteer Voices* of SafePlace, *Savitri* magazine (Bhubaneswar, India), Puja Journal of the Bengali community of Austin, and *Affirming Flame*, *Writings by Progressive Texas Poets in the aftermath of September 11th*, Evelyn Street Press.

I am grateful to Indira Chakravorty not only for the illustrations that give this book its unique look but also for her continuous encouragement and support that made this book possible. I thank Karen J. Wilson and Shamita Das Dasgupta for kindly reading the manuscript and offering their comments for the readers. Lastly, this compilation would not have been possible without the support of my husband Jayadev Misra, that came in countless forms, from putting up with my unconventional work patterns for years, to setting up the computer and devices needed, without being asked.

Many of the poems in this book were inspired by the lives and feelings of survivors of abuse. I hope that colleagues and activists will consider the book as an outreach and fundraising tool to benefit their cause.

Mamata Misra

MOTHER

AND CHILD

A LOVING PRESENCE

They follow me everywhere
when the fragrance of a distant flower
floats in the morning air
when a busy day's chores
leave no moments to spare
when the sun kisses goodbye
to a blushing west sky
in the silence of the night
whether I sleep like a log or sit tight
I know that they are there.

I remember discovering
their presence so loving
when life danced and sang
shaping my womb in its play;
suddenly I felt them watching
from above, behind, and the sides
ceaselessly sending
eternal blessings and love
and I knew that they looked like
my mother's eyes.

CHILD, BEWARE!

One teaches love, the other hate
one unites, the other divides
one enlightens, the other blinds
one reveals, the other conceals
one uplifts, the other pulls down
both walk under the same umbrella
called religion
both may look alike
so, child, beware!
use your 'why's to know which is which
don't mistake the other for the one.

DILEMMA

My babbling baby, my precious jewel
your smile fills my day
but some day, when you ask
who and where your father is
what would I say, I wonder!

Would I smile and try
"Your father the great guy
is working hard far away
will come home one day,"
to keep your smile shining
would I lie, I wonder!

Or would I say with a sigh
"You have only a mother
but you need not bother
you are everything to her
she loves you so much
from here all the way to the sky!"

Or would my face harden
would my speech fail
watching memory play
a scene where your father
couldn't care less
whether we lived or died
I wonder if my stony looks
would steal your smile away!

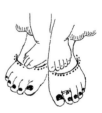

MAYA

What does Maya mean, Mama
you asked me the other day.
What Maya does mean, son
I didn't know how to say.

Should I say …
It's a name for a cause
whose effect you see and feel
in birth, in death, and in life?
It's a name for the power
to create and conceal?
It's Maya's play that makes us forget
that a pot was only clay?

Would it make any sense to say
Maya makes you believe that
'this' is you and 'that' is they
and they are in your way?
Our essence is the same substance
but because of Maya
we hide behind our various kinds
not knowing who we are?

Should I say …
Look, the waves in the ocean
are really shapes of water
All the creatures in this world
are not separate from their creator!
Hidden from your Self
you think you are your ego;
that's what Maya does so well
should I say and let it go?

If I say any of this
would you understand
or would you think your Mama
is really out of her mind?
Not knowing what to say
I said, "We'll talk another day."
Pondering deep into your question
I silently drove away.

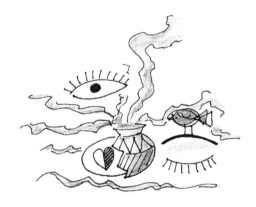

DOUBLE GAP

Why can't we talk, mother and child?
Is it only because we are different?
Everything about me
is from another time and place
except my nationality.
Everything about you
is from here and now
except your looks.
But should that matter?

A child about your age
said to me today
"I liked the way you talked
with us, not *to* us."
Why can't I talk *with* you?
What stands in our way?

When I was a child
I learnt a mother tongue
to talk with my mother
and all the others.
Today that tongue takes charge
when I do something
basic like counting
or intimate like loving
or automatic like warning to prevent an accident
or praying desperately
or when my feelings are too intense.

But for you there was no mother tongue
in the air to absorb.
So I tried to learn a child tongue
and struggled as it changed
from the twos through the teens
and much I still don't know.

Yet, what if we don't speak
the same mother tongue?
If I can talk with others
speaking your tongue,
why can't I talk with you?

A MOTHER'S PLEA

You wish
things were different
I was there for you when you needed
our home was intact, your life normal
so do I.

But in life's journey, you and I have to walk
together or alone, with our own feet
streets are one-way, there is no turning back
some roads are paved, some rough
some are lighted, some dark
sometimes one can see, other times not
but one has to move on, can't stop
maps are rather sketchy
streets aren't marked well
any turn is one's best guess
one can never for sure know
where another path would have led.

Children think that parents know it all
you followed me believing
that I knew where I was going
that I would carry you in my arms uphill
how could you have known
that I would stumble and fall
that my arms would break and legs stall
making it impossible to carry you along
I didn't know either.

Thank God someone was there
to carry you along a brighter path.
Now our paths meet again
you, as tall as I, not needing my arms
together or alone we can walk
but if we choose to walk together for a while
in a path, smooth or rough, lighted or dark

why not smile, why not chat?
why let anger, blame, and silence walk between us
making us distant strangers?
why not let the blood that flows within
bring us closer?

WAR AND PEACE

SEPTEMBER ELEVEN, TWO THOUSAND ONE

One wakes up to find two skyscraping chimneys
shooting dark clouds up a clear blue Manhattan sky.
As sips of coffee shake off the remains of the night's sleep
the chimneys strangely resemble the twin towers.

A horror movie? One wonders
why so early in the morning?
Squinted eyeballs open into a wide awe
as giant mushroom ash clouds (from an invisible rocket?)
engulf the city of NY.

The TV replays again and again to convince one
of the easy descent of a tower
a floor at a time, like an elevator.
One still doesn't know that
the things one saw thrown out the windows
were people jumping off the high floors
for their last breath of air.

Noise and chaos, fire and smoke
charred skin and detached limbs
broken glass and flying debris
fear and desperation mingle in the air.
One asks one's own sense
what's fragile, what's secure?

Twin follows twin
and others give in.

Airplane passengers gone with the flame
smoked streets, trapped workers
struggling firefighters, dazed survivors
uniformed helpers, crowded hospitals
generous blood donors
unfinished conversations
grieving souls, anxious loved ones

grounded transports, stuck passengers
reports of a stunned, stalled America in prayer
blend with the minutes and hours into the dusk.

Does the setting sun miss two tall mirrors
as its flaming reflections
tower over the calm bay waters
as if nothing much has happened?

A ghost of a city sighs deep smoky breaths
not knowing how many thousands, alive or dead
spend the night under the mountain of rubbles.
If tonight isn't known, what does one know
of the days, months, and years to come?

Smoke swirls into the holes in the sky
confirming what one knows
how an hour of war kills years of peace
but concealing what one doesn't know
how years of insane hate create that horrible hour.

LETTER FROM EXILE

Mother dear
your arms that held me with love
have frozen.
They won't hug me again.
Your fingers
whose magic touch could heal my pain
hang heavy
unable to wipe away my tears.

From your safe shelter
you pushed me
untrained, weaponless
to fight a lost battle, to be a prisoner.
After a narrow escape
as I struggle to survive
I ask for a little empathy.
But you offer me
punishment to fit the crime
of innocence.
Exile!
What else?

To my misery, you add
the burden of your castle of lies
where I am not your daughter
given away and returned back
battered and thrown out
divorced and living alone
but your daughter
a traditional wife
a proud mother of a precious son
living happily with her husband
in a distant wonderland!

You can't understand
why my broken arms
don't hold up your dream castle
to protect you from the shame
of my wish to live
as a human being!

I can't understand
why your fear of what people will say
rules over the love for your child
and your sense of right and wrong.
Closing your eyes on her plight
closing your ears on her words
closing your heart on her pain
you close your door on her face!
How severe must be this fear
that numbs a mother's melting heart
into a rock!

I don't know if you will ever understand
yet, it is so simple to see
why one would rather be free from slavery
why one would rather live
with human dignity
than die with false respectability!

Mother dear,
my struggle and your fear
I don't know when they will end.
Someday, I pray, you can see and feel
I can forget and forgive
and we both can be at peace.

NIGHTMARE IN DAYLIGHT

Hindus and Muslims
refusing to share health and happiness
turn into demons burning each other alive.
Their half burnt bodies lying wall to wall
on the same hospital floor
share grief and misery.
The rest of their bodies
turn into dark smelly smoke
sharing the sky of Ahmedabad.
No one notices this irony
as the nightmare continues.

WAR AND PEACE

We pray …
sarve bhavantu sukhinah (may all be happy)
sarve santu niraamayaah (may all be safe)
sarve bhadraani pashyantu (may all see prosperity)
maa kashchit duhkhabhaak bhavet (may no one suffer pain)
om shantih, shantih, shantih (peace, peace, peace!)

But how can one be happy and safe
see prosperity not suffering
when it is war, war, war?

War, war, war!
shock and awe!
power of weapons
of precise destruction
or perhaps not so precise?

What does a mother say
to the child she tucks in bed
not knowing who will be
the night's collateral?

COLLATERAL DAMAGE

I used to talk with elementary school kids
about alternatives to bullying.
I used to chat with middle school kids
about resolving conflicts in relationships
without hurting someone.
I used to discuss with high school kids
that violence is
to use one's power
to control another
physically
or psychologically.
I used to emphasize
the importance
of respect and equality
of justice and peace
for all.

Now our esteemed leaders
have shown by example
that it is okay to bully
that conflicts cannot be resolved
without use of weapons
that it is necessary to use your power
to control others physically
and psychologically
that you need not respect those
you consider insignificant and unequal
that power of domination
rules and defines
necessity, security, justice and peace
the way it pleases.

My collateral damage
is invalidation
of my past occupation
the future of our kids
and the present pause
in the meditation for
peace, peace, peace.

INVOCATION

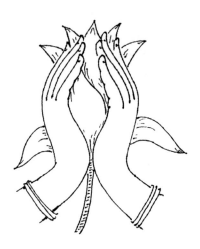

Peace! Come to us!
Calm our noise with your silence!
Cool our simmering hearts to stand still!
Guide us to delve deep into our hearts
for compassion!
Remove our walls of pain and prejudices!
Let our minds mingle free!
Peace! Come to us! Open our eyes!
Lead us from darkness to light.

QUESTIONS

NOT ANSWERS

WOMAN

She is not an idol made of clay or stone
She is not a goddess seated on a throne
She is just like us made of blood and flesh
She has basic needs like everyone else

She is not a Seetha she isn't from a story
Not fire-born Dhraupadhi she needs no glory
Fire burns her body, just like mine, and yours
She is just a woman she wants what is hers

She is not an item she has no owner
How come she is given away by a donor?
Marriage is a means; it is not the end!
She can be an ally; she can be a friend!

In a lifelong journey she can share the load!
Why make her a burden, then leave on the road?
She isn't a slave; she does not need a master
Wants a friend to walk beside, not run past her

Mother made by Nature, children she must raise.
Higher than the Heaven? Overstated praise!
She is only human has no godly power.
She can't bring bad luck good luck she can't shower.

If she's not a goddess must she be a witch?
Is she less than human pushed into a ditch?
Why can't we all see this ridiculous mess?
There's no witch or goddess just woman speechless

Why isn't she sent to school just like her brother?
Marriage is a means for him but end for her?
Why is he raised an asset she a burden?
She an unpaid gardener he owns the garden!

We are like flamingos standing on one foot!
Eyes closed, head tucked! Can we change our attitude?

LOST OR FOUND?

I have escaped a concentration camp!
I am in one piece, safe, free!
I can sleep when I like
get up when I want to and do as I wish.
No one will order me with an *or else* cane.
No one will control my life
by the hour, minute, and second again.
I have freedom, freedom at last!
Freedom to celebrate, cherish, enjoy!
I should be dancing with joy!

Yet, I feel
empty, lonely, deprived
cheated out of life!
My future appears to be a desert
stretching out to the end of the world!
I pine to shower my love to turn it green
but how can I?

I ask a million questions for which
there are no answers.
Why did my dream home
turn into a concentration camp?
Why did my Dr. Jekyll turn into Mr. Hyde?
Surely he is going to change back, won't he?
The anguish, the pain, would it ever go away?
I treasure fond memories
of dear sweet Dr. Jekyll.
Why did he leave me?
I love him, married
to grow old with him
to live with him until death.
Had he died, perhaps I would grieve
and then accept my destiny!
But he is here, playing hide and seek
with my mind.

Why? I am tired of searching.
Pulled by Dr. Jekyll
and pushed away by Mr. Hyde
my mind is torn into pieces.
So confused!

How long, O God,
can I go on like this?
Please help me see
that I am not a loser
how could I have lost
what I never had?
I am a winner, won my freedom, didn't I?
The past was all pain, future uncertain
God, help me live in the present
to build a future on the foundation of
my new found freedom and strength.

PUZZLE

Path is dirty and wet
from Start to Finish.
Feet must walk all the way
without getting dirty.
Those are the rules of the game.

Hmm, what to do?
Puzzled feet look up to us.
We hand them the obvious clue.
Shoes! You can wear shoes.

Of course!
Dancing happily
feet slip into dainty shoes
for protection
and buckle up for security
and take a few cautious steps.
Somehow it doesn't feel quite right.
But it's too late when they discover
that the shoes are made of mud!

What to do now? Worried, distressed
they look up to us again for answers.
It's your problem!
Don't look at us!
We retort this time.
If you don't sweat
your shoes won't get wet.
Remember, it's only natural
for dry mud to get muddy when wet
but it's your job to stay clean
from Start to Finish and
win the medal of honor.
If you fail and be a loser
shame on you!

Does this sound familiar,
good women, men, people?

QUESTIONS TO NIRMALA

Why, Nirmala, why?
Was it the only way?

You searched for six years for a solution!
But bullets won over all other options
your upbringing wouldn't allow.
You would rather be dead than divorced!
Your kids would rather be dead than orphans!

Is that the Indian way?
What do you say?

Why did you ask the finder of your note
to send the contents of your safe deposit box
to your mother?
Was that a gesture of your anger against
the society that shamelessly treats females
as merchandise?
What were you trying to say?

And now, does your soul care how
people interpret what you so strongly
tried to assert?

As an unfortunate incident to be forgotten,
as a crazy woman's inhuman act,
or as a big bold question mark
on those Indian values
that you paid such a high price
to preserve?

DOORMAT TO JACKPOT

He smiles at me.
He says, "Whatever you wish, darling!"
He asks, "What do you think?"
He cares about how I feel!
He says, "You are tired!
Why not rest a while?"
His voice so soft!
He lends a helping hand!
He puts his arms around me.
His touch gentle!
A man can be so loving?
I thought all men were like the one
for whom I was just a doormat!
And now, when I hear
"I hit the jackpot, honey!"
am I dreaming? I wonder
how can it be?
The same old me
a doormat for one and
a jackpot for another?

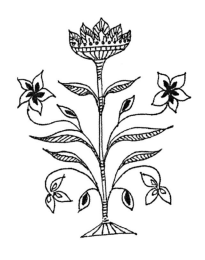

HOPE AND DESPAIR

POVERTY LINE

It's not that I don't have, I do.
A decent annual family income
a luxury car, a nice modern apartment
health insurance, a bank account
a phone card, a credit card, a computer
all these belong to
the community of marriage, ours,
a nice concept!

I also have strict orders
not to use
central heating or cooling
dishwasher, computer
check book, credit card, dollars.
So I secretly save pennies
to trade in for something I may need.

Orders clearly say not to
call my mother,
drive the family car
see a doctor, buy pain killers
check mail, ask questions
give answers, earn money
or make friends.

So I secretly ride
the number 44 bus
wherever it takes me
and scribble something
on some application form
hoping that someone will call me
soon for a job interview.

The order is the law!
If I disobey, who knows
what else will break?

So I secretly pray
for a miracle to happen
silently walking on
that fine line between
what I have and have not
what I can and cannot.

WINTER BLOSSOMS

The red bud tree in my back yard
is dressed in bright pink
fooled by the unusual mid-January warmth.
Surely it's spring, it says.
The weatherman shakes his head.
The Alaskan front is days away
from stripping off that beautiful attire.

Malathi, when you say
Surely he is going to change
when he sees his baby kick and cry
and touches the tender skin!
After all, isn't it his own flesh and blood!
when you try not to remember
how he left you to bleed alone, to starve
not caring if his baby in your womb
kicked or not,
I feel like the weatherman,
knowing that the battering front
is only days away
from turning your hope into despair.

TO THE AUTUMN MOON

Singing silly songs that make little sense
the little girl worships your fullness
not knowing the cause for celebration.
Your silky soft light soothes
her fear of dark night
playing an enchanting sight
of shadows and light
waking her dreamy imagination.

Tomorrow she will dance
to your rhythm, to your call
slowly she will know
how intimate is this relation.
But Autumn Moon,
don't wait for tomorrow;
tell her today before she succumbs
to silence, dependence, and submission.

Tell her not to hide
urge her to look inside
to see that like you she too can make tide;
and you will have her smile of appreciation.

GOODBYE, FEAR

Late last night, you came
wearing the costume of a nightmare.
Not knowing from whom, I fled.
Locking myself in a closet
hiding behind the clothes
I shrank, not wanting to be seen.
I remained squatted
for a long time
before I noticed I wasn't alone
I had company of a sister.
Perhaps she was afraid too
perhaps not
I wouldn't know because I didn't ask
I couldn't let go of silence.
I couldn't see if you had left
I didn't open my eyes
holding on to darkness.

I woke up feeling
your foot prints on a burning stomach
your finger marks on a knotted chest.
My hair stretched to catch
bones trembled to blend
a still chill you had left in the air.

I see you again and again
in hiding faces
in silent voices
in passive steps.
But I know that you leave
when courage dawns.
A safe space warms your chill
time loses your prints
faces smile, voices speak
and steps slowly but surely
lead to peace.

DREAMS, NIGHTMARES, AND REALITY

Love and affection, hope and protection
I thought I saw in the hand
I held with trust, without hesitation
to come to this faraway land.

It was just an illusion not a clear vision
It melted away and is gone.
My body is battered; dreams are shattered
I have no one to lean on.

Dreams are gone never to return
nightmares have taken their place
where I run through a maze with absolute craze
as every door closes on my face.

I stretch my hands to catch a rope ladder
that hangs above my head
But it turns into a noose around my neck
and says, "They want you dead!"

"No, no, no, no, let me out of here,
let me out of here," I cry.

Then I wake up with a pounding heart
and a mouth very dry.

Pulling myself up, sipping water from a cup
I think about my dream.
My maze is so real; it's my ordeal
it does me no good just to scream.

I mustn't run wild, can't afford to feel tired
every maze has a way out!
Efforts well-thought, battles well-fought
bring some good results about!

I must look at my options, avoid distractions
and pick a path that seems the best.
If it goes nowhere, I would backtrack and turn
to find a new path to try next.

The soft flowing water in a long river
finds its final destination
through the tall mountains and the wide plains
it travels all the way to the ocean.

When my fate presents unexpected events
barriers that block my way
I can go around not just round and round
riding my own free will away.

UNSPOKEN WORDS

When thunder strikes
I shut my eyes tight
and cover my ears
hoping it would disappear.

But lightening draws
sharp red curves
in the dark skies
of the vast universe
behind my closed eyes.

Before I know
rain pours in tears
washing away
the unspoken words
back to the bottom of the pit
breaking off that stairwell
they had painfully climbed
to reach the tip of my tongue.

DESPAIR

A gentle touch on the shoulder
a twinkling smile
a soft whisper in the ear
a nod of understanding
a hand to hold
a caring word
a shoulder to cry on
a pair of arms holding tight
a warm kiss
devoid of all this
the soul slowly fades away
leaving the ghost
of a love-thirsty body
numb to all desires.
After a life-long search
for crumbs of love
in all reachable corners
in all possible ways
even thirst has left
in despair.

MEDICINE FOR HIM TO CURE HER DEPRESSION

Warning:
Start immediately.
Do not freeze or refrigerate.
Store in a warm place.
Do not discontinue.
Do not skip a dose.
If no improvement is noticed after two months,
consult your doctor.

Dosage:
Twice daily, morning and bed time.

Direction:
Morning time:
    Hold her hands for one minute.
    Look into her eyes.
    Say, "Take care."

Bed time:
    Hold her in your arms
    for one minute.
    Ask, "How do you feel?"
    Listen to her response.
    Then say, "I love you."

Side effects on him:
Awkwardness, shyness, anxiety or an uneasy feeling are common, at least initially.
If these side effects continue after two months, consult your doctor.

Side effects on her:
Resistance, disbelief, crying, sobbing, skepticism, and anger are common, at least
initially. They go away as the medicine starts working. If these side effects persist
after two months, consult your doctor.

Not a substitute for her prescription medicine. If in doubt, consult your doctor.

HOPE

The ember slowly burns into ashes
where a bright flame once danced
in flying colors.
Is this what life is all about?
I hear obscure words
"You are immortal!" they say
How can there be nectar
where there isn't even water?
"You are fullness!" they say
But I feel empty!
I don't get it, am I dumb?
"You are knowledge!" they say
Speechless, I can only
sigh with disbelief
making the ember glow.
A flow of breeze
from the right direction
could make it a blazing flame!

A SIMPLE MISTAKE

After the long ritual where
our hands were tied together in an irreversible knot
to last a lifetime
after the age-old mantras were chanted
with sacred fire as witness
pronouncing us husband and wife
after we took seven steps forward together
to a point of no return
after we assured the North Star that
our commitment was just as true and firm
after a few hundred people were fed
and an equal number of gifts accepted
after my parents exchanged a lifetime's savings
for a new happy life for me
after I said good-bye to
my dear ones with teary eyes
knowing that the place I left
would never be my home again
after I was welcomed into your family
where we offered together to your ancestors
rice balls cooked by me

after distinguishing symbols of the married state
decorated my face, draped my body,
and braced my wrists, fingers, ankles, and toes
after my virginity was asked for, given, and taken
after I got used to calling a new name mine
after I started worshipping you as I was taught to do
after my commitment turned into my first love
after I poured my heart into making a new home with you

you say it was a mistake
a simple mistake that you regret
that should not have happened
but can easily be fixed
like saying sorry and hanging up
after dialing a wrong number
like returning the wrong shirt
you bought by mistake
all that needs to be done is
signing some papers for a simple no-fault divorce
for marrying the wrong woman.
Who said marriage is irreversible?
The law says married until divorced or dead.
And the rituals? I could forget them
like those doll weddings in a child's play.
Couldn't I?

Your male privilege blinds you from seeing
that when your d-word would push me down
from married space
to a socially undefined space
Sage Society would yell
"Don't come back; hold it right there"
making me hang in mid-space
like a Trishanku.

SOUND

AND SILENCE

WRITER'S COMPANION

You never complain
when I drag you out of bed
in the middle of the night.
You don't ask with sleepy eyes
"Can't we wait till morning?"

You're patient like the earth
when my uncontrollable urge
like lava from a volcano
covers you in layers
one pushing another
before it has a chance
to cool down and take shape.

You stay calm and wait
when I just sit and stare
my thoughts waiting to ride
an expression stalled somewhere.
You must have seen those clouds
one can't tell when they'd rain.

You don't resist when I try
new makeovers on you
with colors of words
strokes of lines
shadows of ideas
and a touch of punctuation
here and there.
You never say, "That's enough"
when I try one last time again.

Not judging
you pay attention to all I say.
Like a mirror you reflect,
"Here, dear, this is what you say."
"Is this how you feel?"
"Is that what you mean?"

And it is okay with you
whatever I choose to do
keep it the same or change
erase, start over, or forget
keep it a secret, or share.

ROLLERCOASTER

I ride the rollercoaster
of my thoughts
an unpredictable ride
full of sudden twists and turns
and ups and downs.

The free falls scare me
"Never again!" I tell myself
but until the next fall I am unaware
that I am riding the rollercoaster again.

But now I have a clue on
how to tell a harmless thought
from one that may be a deadly trap.
If it has an "I" or a "me" in it
chances are that it is the killer kind.

CONTEMPLATION

Please accept me as I am!
I am unable to guess your mood
or read your mind,
to smile, talk sweet, or always be kind.
But I try, I love, and I care.
I am human just as you are.
Why can't you just let me be?
If I can accept your usual silence,
why can't you accept my occasional sound?

The wounded ego, wild and wary,
finds faded fragments from memory.
Past events that had given pain,
come alive and hurt over again.

Luckily, wisdom comes to rescue.
Wake up, dreamer, who are you?
Look at yourself; see who you are!
You need no one to let you be!
You are! You already are! Don't you see?
Your maker accepts you as you are.
Dwell on that! That you are!

OUTSIDE THE ICU WINDOW

People gather for *darshan*.
Some have traveled for hours.
A kind guard lifts the curtains
to unveil a battleground
where life meets death.
They stand on their toes
to take a peek
not only at the helpless body
of someone they love
but also at their own future.
Curtains drop and silently they turn
wondering why it couldn't be easier
like a river meeting the ocean
or a ripe fruit falling.

PRINCESS

Here she lies
not a worry in the world
a dozen or more at her service
to oil, bathe, and powder
to clean, and dress her
to massage her feet
to feed special meals
to read and sing to her
without her lifting a finger.
But neither can she see
nor command those eager souls
lining up to serve her.
The price of royal treatment!

MORE ICU SCRIBBLES

ICU, I see you again and again
intensely, carefully
the hallway to your unit
wet with tears, soft with love
heavy with anxiety
bound with duty
noisy with questions
silent with answers
awaits with patience
for the unknown
as a numb witness
watches Kali dance
with Kala flowing
a moment at a time
into eternity.

A SPACE EULOGY

A dance to the music of time
on the stage of space
with stars as the back drop
has come to an abrupt end!
The dancers didn't choose
the music or the ending
only the songs of their dreams
and the steps of astro science.

Is the dance over?
When the dancers became one
with the earth we walk on
the air we breathe in
didn't they pass on
their dreams, their songs,
their passion, their aspiration
to our young?
You cannot choose
when you are going to die or how
but you can decide
how you are going to live now.

SILENCE

Desirable when sound is not
in prayer
in meditation
in search into one's soul
in firm understanding
in ecstasy beyond sound's reach

But when silence steals sound's place
giving varying messages
from "I don't know"
or "I don't care"
to "Don't you dare!"
is it silence
or is it something else
wearing a mask of silence?

If you let sound and silence trade places
what do you get as consequence?

NOCTURNAL THOUGHTS

Unpredictable, unfair,
unforgiving, unkind,
harsh utterance of
a self-centered psyche
sharpened with anger,
jealousy, and pain
pierces with ease,
a presumably dense,
sophisticated wall
of understanding
and tolerance,
proving it inapt
to protect the fragile,
frail, fearful feelings.

OPPORTUNITY

The qualities you admired one day
are the same ones that anger you today!
Lucky is the one who survived
both your praise and rage.
She got the opportunity to see
how opposites can only be
as far from each other
as the faces of a coin.

MATRIMONIAL

It said:
bride needed
for a charming
young man
with a good salary
Must be good looking
and from a good family

It didn't say
but you should have known anyway:

efficient
to run the house with little money
fast learner
to cook just like her mother-in-law
discrete
to not ask annoying questions
grateful
for her good fortune
smart
to know how to dress for the right occasion
content
to stay home and make it sweet
happy with herself
not needing to visit or phone friends

pure in heart
not seeking attention from other men
traditional homemaker
not wanting to work outside the home
strong
to take an occasional beating now and then
loving
to lie and die for her husband when asked.

SILENT WITNESSES

Silently they see
what we do, what we don't.
Silently they say
what we didn't, what we couldn't.
Silently they suggest
what we can, what we must.
Their silence gives us
a new voice, a different choice.
Let their silent presence guide us.

RIGHTS

Your rights are like Lakshmi
knowing them is Saraswati
living them is Shakti, sister,
the goddesses are with you.

IN TRANSITION

Golden gown fallen,
bashful bare brown body begs
a silver cover.

ON ENCHANTED ROCK

Wind blew through my ears
"I am your first and last friend,"
It yelled, "Do you hear?"

POEMS

AND PEOPLE

POEMS

A Loving Presence was felt in 1977 and remained in the subconscious until it transformed into a poem around 1995 and appeared in an anthology produced by the Chinmaya Mission of Austin. It changed considerably for inclusion in this book. It has always been a tribute to my mother.

Child, Beware! was written in 2002 and appeared in a newsletter of the Chinmaya Mission of Austin.

Dilemma was written in 1999 and appeared in the SAHELI Newsletter in 2005.

Maya was born in 1993 after my son and I attended an inspiring talk by Maya Angelou. It appeared in the Journal of the Orissa Society of the Americas in its original form. It has changed quite a bit since then.

Double Gap was written in 1995.

A Mother's Plea was written in 1998.

September Eleven, Two Thousand One was born from the restlessness of the day. It appeared in the webzine South Asian Womens' Forum at www.sawf.org in 2001 and was published in *Affirming Flame, Writings by Progressive Texas Poets in the aftermath of September 11th*, Evelyn Street Press, Austin, Texas, 2002.

Letter from Exile was written in 1997 and appeared in the SAHELI Newsletter in 1998.

Nightmare in Daylight was born from the restlessness of the communal violence in India in 2002 and appeared in the SAHELI Newsletter in 2003.

War and Peace was written in 2003 when the Iraq war started. The peace prayer in the first verse is in Sanskrit language and is a common Hindu prayer.

Collateral Damage was written in 2003 when the Iraq war started. It appeared in the SAHELI Newsletter in 2004.

Invocation was written in 2001 for a peace event after the 911 attack.

I wrote **Woman** initially in 1994 in Oriya, my mother tongue and first language. Later, in 1995, I rewrote it in English and it appeared in the Asian American Quarterly, an Austin based publication, in 1997.

Seetha (also spelled Seeta, or Sita) is a female character in the Indian epic Ramayana. Her husband, king Rama, rescued her from her kidnapper Ravana by defeating him in a war. After the rescue, Rama, who put his duty as a king before his personal happiness, felt a moral dilemma to accept Seetha back as his wife, fearing objection from the citizens. Seetha walked into fire to prove her chastity. Fire did not burn her, certifying her purity, qualifying her to be the queen, and ruling out any probable future objection from the citizens.

Dhroupadhi, daughter of king Dhrupadha and a central character in the Indian epic Mahabharata, was born out of fire during a ritual performed by her father and therefore was immune to harm by fire.

In India, a significantly large number of women die of fire-related injuries; while some of these deaths are accidental, many turn out to be suicide or murder.

Swami, the word for husband in many Indian languages, also means master.

"Mother and motherland are greater than the heaven" is a quote from the epic Ramayana that has been quoted often and may have conditioned us. A woman who has little power as a daughter or wife may gain power by virtue of her motherhood. Sometimes she exerts her power over her son to oppress her daughter-in-law.

Lost or Found? was written in 1997.

Puzzle was written in 2004 and appeared in the SAHELI Newsletter in 2005.

I wrote **Questions to Nirmala** in 1996 after reading a disturbing article titled 'When Hope Dies' on the Houston Chronicle, July 7, 1996. The story was about an extreme case of domestic violence in a South Asian family. According to the story, on March 22, 1996, Nirmala Katta of Houston had killed her abusive husband of eight years, her three children of ages six, five, and two, set fire to their house, and killed herself. In addition to being abusive, her husband had intimate relationships with four other women while he was married to Nirmala. Although Nirmala repeatedly asked her family to help her, she never went to any mainstream battered women's organization for help. There were no South Asian anti-domestic violence organizations in Houston at that time. The story validated my work with SAHELI and urged me to do more community outreach and domestic violence prevention education. The poem appeared in DAYA Newsletter in Houston a few years later. It also got translated into Oriya and appeared in a magazine called Savitri in Bhubaneswar, India.

Doormat to Jackpot was written in 2002.

Poverty Line was written in 2002 and appeared in the SAHELI Newsletter in 2003.

Winter Blossoms came about in January 1999 and appeared in the SAHELI Newsletter the same year.

It came out rather unexpectedly. Early one morning, I pulled the blinds on the kitchen window and saw the red bud tree in our back yard full of blossoms overnight. I remembered the weather forecast from the night before and at the same time saw the face of a woman I had been helping superimposed on the tree branches. It was one of those moments when I have to surrender myself to the writing urge that takes control of me. I found myself typing away at the computer instead of pouring myself some coffee.

To the Autumn Moon was written in 1996 for reading at a gathering on the occasion of Kumar Purnima, an autumn moon festival celebrated by the Oriya community of Texas.

Goodbye, Fear was born after a nightmare in 1999. It appeared in Volunteer Voices, a newsletter for the volunteers of Safe Place, Austin.

Dreams, Nightmares, and Reality was written in 1993 marking my first exposure to a battered woman from my community in the US. It also coincided with my decision to join SAHELI and commit myself to its cause, which would change my life forever. The poem appeared in the Journal of the Orissa Society of the Americas in 1994.

Unspoken Words came about spontaneously in 1997 after I attended a court hearing where a tape of verbal abuse was played. It appeared in the SAHELI Newsletter in 1998.

Despair was written in 1997. I was helping a friend suffering from an acute depression at the time.

Medicine for Him to Cure Her Depression was written in 1997. It appeared in the SAHELI Newsletter in 2000.

Hope was written in 1997.

A Simple Mistake was written in 1999 after I watched a young woman abandoned and divorced soon after her marriage. It appeared in the DAYA Newsletter in 1999 and in the South Asian Women's Forum webzine www.sawf.org in 2000. Trishanku, mentioned in the poem, is a mythological character. According to Indian mythology, a man named Trishanku gained godhood by virtue of his good deeds and was raised to Heaven. But when Trishanku was about to reach Heaven, a god who saw Trishanku as a threat pushed him down. As Trishanku began falling down toward Earth, the great sage Biswamitra, who had helped him rise up, yelled, "Don't Fall. Stay where you are." The power struggle between the god and the sage left Trishanku hanging in the middle space below Heaven and above Earth.

Writer's Companion was written in 1999. It appeared in Scribe, the Quarterly Journal of the Austin Writers' League in 2000.

Rollercoaster was written in 1993.

Contemplation was written in 1993. It appeared in a journal of the Austin Chinmaya Mission in 1996.

Outside the ICU Window was written in 2002 when I was attending to my mother-in-law in the hospital. It appeared in the Journal of the Orissa Society of the Americas in 2003. The word *darshan* is used in most north Indian languages to mean viewing of someone revered like a god, a king, a guru, or someone special.

Princess was written in 2002 when I was taking care of my mother-in-law, left blind and unconscious after a stroke.

More ICU Scribbles was written in 2003 when I was attending to my aunt in the hospital. Kali is a Hindu goddess in a dark and violent form symbolizing annihilation. She also represents the source of creative power and is worshipped

as the benevolent mother-goddess. Kala is the name of the Hindu god symboliz-
ing time.

A Space Eulogy was written in 2003 after a spacecraft accident that killed all the
astronauts aboard.

Silence was written in 2006. I wrote it for a workshop I was co-facilitating at the
ACT Summit I, held in Atlanta, Georgia. ACT (Action + Community = Trans-
formation) is a national team working to develop intervention and prevention
strategies to end child sexual abuse in the South Asian communities in the US.

Nocturnal Thoughts was written in 2001.

Opportunity was written in 2002.

Matrimonial was written in 2005.

Silent Witnesses was written in 2000.

Rights was written in 2002. I had participated in a workshop at the University of
Texas called the Austin Project where poets, performing artists, and activists
experimented with Image Theater to sculpt their ideas with human bodies and
expressions and have participants interpret what they saw. The precursor to this
poem was born at the workshop. It was the fall season when Hindu goddesses are
publicly worshipped with grandeur. Within a week, my scribbles from the work-
shop evolved into this poem, retaining only the title. Lakshmi, Saraswati, and
Shakti are names of goddesses worshipped by Hindus for wealth, knowledge, and
strength respectively. In 2004, this poem and its Bengali translation by Indira
Chakravorty appeared in a journal published by the Austin Bengali community
during Durga Pooja, a Hindu festival.

In Transition was written in 1996 in a creative writing class I attended at the
Hyde Park Baptist Church, Austin, taught by Dr. Lillian Brown. It was included
in the class journal.

On Enchanted Rock was written in 1996 after climbing the rock. It was very
windy on the top of the rock.

THE POET

Mamata Misra, a community volunteer and anti-violence activist living in Austin, Texas, is a contributing author in *Affirming Flame, Writings by Progressive Texas Poets in the aftermath of September 11th* (Evelyn Street Press, 2002), in a documentary film *Veil of Silence* (Maitri, 2006), and in various newsletters and journals. She has edited two books, *RISC 6000 Technology* (IBM Corporation, 1990) and *You Can! A Guide for the Immigrant Woman to Live Independently in the US* (SAHELI, 2000). Formerly, the Programs Director of SAHELI, an organization in Austin, Texas that assists Asian families dealing with domestic abuse, Mamata Misra is a core member of a national team called ACT (Action + Community = Transformation) that is developing prevention and intervention strategies for child sexual abuse in the South Asian communities in the US. Her community service has been recognized by many local organizations, including SafePlace with outstanding volunteer awards (1996, 1997, and 1998), India Community Center (2000), the Samaritan Center and the St. Edwards University with the Ethics in Business Finalist award (2004 and 2005), and the YWCA with the Woman of the Year award (2005).

THE ARTIST

Indira Chakravorty, an artist and activist, is a cofounder of SAHELI in Austin, Texas and DAYA, Inc., in Houston, Texas. Former Transitional Housing Coordinator of Maitri, San Jose, California, Indira is the Volunteer Coordinator at CORA: Community Overcoming Relationship Abuse in San Mateo County, California. She is also a core member of the national team ACT that is developing strategies for intervention and prevention of child sexual abuse in the South Asian communities in the US.

978-0-595-44372-7
0-595-44372-9

Printed in the United States
108253LV00007B/22-120/A